# THE LION KIDS BIBLE COMIC

DEDICATED TO
Sarah Sier
Sophie and Marios
Oliver Blair Milton

Copyright © 2019 The Edge Group
This edition copyright © 2019 Lion Hudson IP Limited

The right of The Edge Group, Mychailo Kazybrid, Bambos Georgiou, Ed Chatelier, Jesus Barony and Jeff Anderson to be identified as the author, inker, colourists, and letterer of this work has been asserted by them in accordance with the Copyright, Designs and Patents Act 1988.

All rights reserved. No part of this publication may be reproduced or transmitted in any form or by any means, electronic or mechanical, including photocopy, recording, or any information storage and retrieval system, without permission in writing from the publisher.

Published by **Lion Children's**
www.lionhudson.com
Part of the SPCK Group
SPCK, 36 Causton Street, London, SW1P 4ST

ISBN 978 0 7459 7719 5
First edition 2019

A catalogue record for this book is available from the British Library
Printed and bound in Poland, July 2021, LH60

# THE LION KIDS BIBLE COMIC

Mychailo Kazybrid with Bambos Georgiou, Jesus Barony, and Jeff Anderson

LION CHILDREN'S

# INTRODUCTION

## IS IT A BIRD, A PLANE ...NO, IT IS THE *LION KIDS BIBLE COMIC!*

Welcome to *The Lion KBC*, putting the 'Joy' into Bible reading. After all, the Bible contains the ultimate GOOD NEWS, and this collection of stories from the Old and New Testaments all hint at the greater joy that is to come.

*The Lion KBC* is designed to make the reading of the Bible fun, engaging and easy to read in a comic-strip format that even the most reluctant readers enjoy. Each panel has been lovingly created, including riddles and humorous features that make the people and stories of the Bible as memorable as popular comic characters and stories.

The team of creators were inspired by their love of comic books and the desire to communicate the Bible to this new generation of young readers still enjoying comic classics from *The Beano* to *Marvel*, and much-loved characters such as Asterix, Tintin and Dennis the Menace.

The creative team includes some of the best Comic creators of the world including: MYCHAILO KAZYBRID - *Wallace and Gromit*, *The Tick* and *Marvel UK*, JEFF ANDERSON - *Transformers* and *Lion Hero Bible*, BAMBOS GEORGIOU - *Marvel* and *DC Comics* and JESUS BARONY - *Bande Dessinee* and *Aces Week*.

To Eternity and beyond!

# CONTENTS

## OLD TESTAMENT

Big Boss . . . . . . . . . . . . . . . . 8
GENESIS 1

Dust Man . . . . . . . . . . . . . . . 9
GENESIS 1, 2

Eve . . . . . . . . . . . . . . . . . . 10
GENESIS 2, 3

Mr Nasty . . . . . . . . . . . . . . 11
GENESIS 3

Cain the Pain . . . . . . . . . . . 12
GENESIS 4

Over the Rainbow . . . . . . . 13
GENESIS 8, 9

Tower of Babel . . . . . . . . . 14
GENESIS 11

B.I.G . . . . . . . . . . . . . . . . . 15
GENESIS 12-14

Wild Boy . . . . . . . . . . . . . . 16
GENESIS 15, 16, 19

Laughter Boy . . . . . . . . . . 17
GENESIS 21-22, 24

Jacob the Dodger . . . . . . . 18
GENESIS 24-25, 27

Uncle Laban . . . . . . . . . . . 20
GENESIS 29-31

Wrestling Superstars . . . . . 21
GENESIS 32

Joseph and the . . . . . . . . . 22
Multicoloured Cape
GENESIS 32, 39, 40

Dream Boy . . . . . . . . . . . . 23
GENESIS 39, 40-41

Governor . . . . . . . . . . . . . 24
GENESIS 42-50

Water Baby . . . . . . . . . . . 25
EXODUS 1-2

Prince of Egypt . . . . 26
EXODUS 2

Wreck It Moses . . . . . . . . . 27
EXODUS 3-6

Great Escape . . . . . . . . . . 29
EXODUS 7-12

Red Sea Crossing . . . . . . . 30
EXODUS 13-14

Chased... and Manna . . . . . . 31
EXODUS 14-16

The Ten Commandments . . . 32
EXODUS 19-40

Promised Land or Bust . . . . 33
NUMBERS 21-22, DEUTERONOMY 34

Josh the Bosh . . . . . . . . . . 34
JOSHUA 1, 3, 5

Wall-E . . . . . . . . . . . . . . . 35
JOSHUA 2, 6

Bash Saint Boys . . . . . . . . 36
JUDGES 1, 3-4, 6-7, 10

Gideon and the . . . . . . . . 38
Desert Raiders
JUDGES 10

# OLD TESTAMENT CONT.

Desperate Sam ............ 39
JUDGES 13-16

Ruth .................... 41
RUTH 1-4

Job ..................... 42
JOB 1-2, 42

Samuel .................. 43
1 SAMUEL 1-4

A King .................. 44
1 SAMUEL 7-8

David, the Shepherd Boy .. 45
1 SAMUEL 16

David and his Catapult ... 46
1 SAMUEL 17-18

Psalm 23 ................ 47
PSALM 23

David Meets Bathsheba ... 48
2 SAMUEL 11-12

Big Heroes .............. 49
2 SAMUEL 23-24

Brainy Solomon .......... 50
1 KINGS 2-3

Solomon's Temple ........ 51
1 KINGS 5-7, 10-11

Wisdom for Life ......... 52
PROVERBS

Queen of Sheba .......... 53
1 KINGS 10

Good, Bad, and Ugly ..... 54
1 KINGS 12-14

Wizzer-Elijah ........... 55
1 KINGS 16-18

Elijah and the .......... 56
Prophets of Baal
1 KINGS 18

Baldy ................... 57
2 KINGS 2

Isaiah - Day of the Lord .. 58
ISAIAH 53

King Hezekiah of Judah ... 59
ISAIAH 6

Josiah, Boy King ........ 60
2 KINGS 22-23

Mr Stubborn ............. 61
JEREMIAH 1, 19-20, 23, 27-29

Chariots of Fire ........ 62
EZEKIEL 1-3, 37, 43-48

Daniel Dare ............. 63
DANIEL 1-2, 6

Temple of Boom .......... 66
EZRA 1, 4

Princess Bride .......... 67
ESTHER 1-8

Jonah the Moaner ........ 68
JONAH 1-4

Lions in the Bible ...... 69
JUDGES 14, ISAIAH 11

Donkeys in the Bible .... 70
NUMBERS 22, LUKE 2, MATTHEW 21

From Old to New ......... 71
MATTHEW 1

Welcome to the .......... 72
New Place
LUKE 1

# NEW TESTAMENT

**Joy Story** . . . . . . . 73
Luke 1:26-38

**Dream Weaver** . . . . . . 75
Matthew 1:18-24, Luke 2:1-8

**Sheep Tales** . . . . . . . 77
Luke 2:8-20

**Annie** . . . . . . . . . . 78
Luke 2:21-38

**Star Trek** . . . . . . . . 79
Matthew 2:1-12

**Nightmare After Christmas** . 81
Matthew 2:13-22

**Home Alone** . . . . . . . 82
Luke 2:41-52

**Hairy Man** . . . . . . . . 83
Matthew 3, 14:1-12

**Temptation of Jesus** . . . 84
Luke 4:1-13

**Calling the Twelve** . . . . 86
Luke 5:1-11

**It's Amazing** . . . . . . . 87
John 2:1-11, Matthew 14:22-33,
John 5:1-15

**More Amazing Stuff** . . . 88
John 9:1-12, Mark 35-41, Luke 7:1-10

**The Big Nosh Up!** . . . . 89
John 6:1-15

**Parables** . . . . . . . . . 90
Luke 15:1-7, 11-31

**Palm Sunday... and a Donkey** 91
Matthew 21:1-17

**Last Supper** . . . . . . . 92
Matthew 26:17-35

**Arrest** . . . . . . . . . . 93
Matthew 26:47-56

**Denial** . . . . . . . . . . 94
Matthew 26:69-75

**Trial** . . . . . . . . . . . 95
Luke 22:66 - 23:25

**Jesus Dies** . . . . . . . . 96
Luke 23:26-47

**Mary Popin** . . . . . . . 97
Luke 24:1-12

**Joy Story 2** . . . . . . . 98
Luke 24:13-35

**Convincing Thomas** . . . 99
John 20:24-29

**Mission Impossible** . . . 101
Acts 1:1-11, 2:5-41

**Inside Out** . . . . . . . . 102
Acts 2:1-4

**Road Runner** . . . . . . . 103
Acts 8:26-40

**Despicable Me** . . . . . . 104
Acts 9:1-31

**Paul's Missionary Journeys** 105
Acts 14:1-20; 27-28; 16:16-40

**Paul's Letters** . . . . . . 108
Acts 28:17-31

**Back to the Future** . . . 109
Revelation 21

In the beginning, God decided that it would be a good idea to create a universe full of wonderful things to see.

So, God began by making the light and the darkness, calling them day and night.

Once God had separated the seas and the land, He enjoyed the grass and the plants.

"That tickles!"

The sun, moon, and the stars were exciting to make.

He filled the water with lots of living creatures and the air with birds.

With the creation of all the animals and humans, it brought things to the 6th day.

Suddenly, God had a great idea for the 7th day...

... a nice long rest!

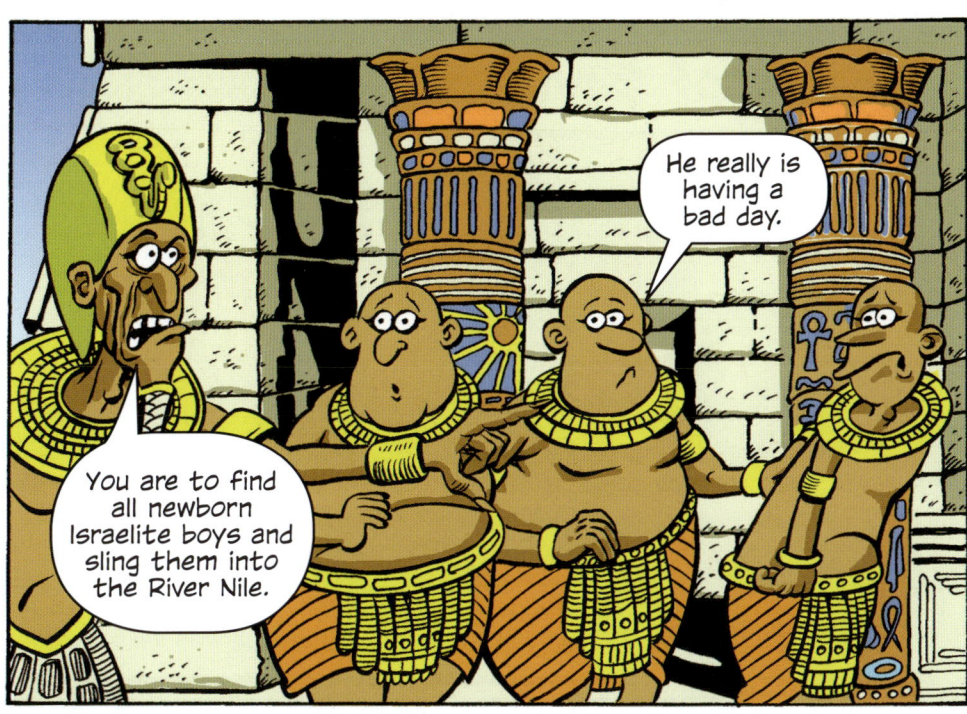

# Psalm 23
written by David

The Lord's my shepherd; I've got everything I need. I can relax in green fields by quiet pools of lovely fresh water.

He helps me to be strong and puts me on the right path.

Even when I go through dark places, God is with me, protecting me with his rod and staff.

He'll prepare a smashing feast with lots of lovely grub and snacks for me; those who don't like me, will press their noses to the windows. He'll fill my cup with my best drinks.

His loving care will be with me all the time, and the door to his house will be for ever open.

# Donkeys in the Bible

Donkeys play a great part in the Bible stories.

Of course, there's the story of how Samson fought lots of Philistines, with only the jawbone of an ex-donkey...

but we'll move on from that.

Moving on, King Balak of the Moabites sent a sorcerer, Balaam, to stop the Israelites, but God made the donkey speak to Balaam.

No way – there's a mean looking chap with wings and flaming sword that looks extra hot.

Are you nuts? There's nobody here, and when exactly were you going to tell me that you could talk?

I don't believe it, I'm talking to a... an angel with a flaming sword.

Hello, sir.

Now, next time, just listen to the donkey.

And so, Balaam decided to bless the Israelites...

... and the donkey never let him get a word in.

Donkeys also had a big part to play in God's plan, from taking Mary and Joseph to Bethlehem to give birth to the baby, Jesus...

... to a donkey carrying Jesus into Jerusalem on the day known as Palm Sunday to the Passover festival.

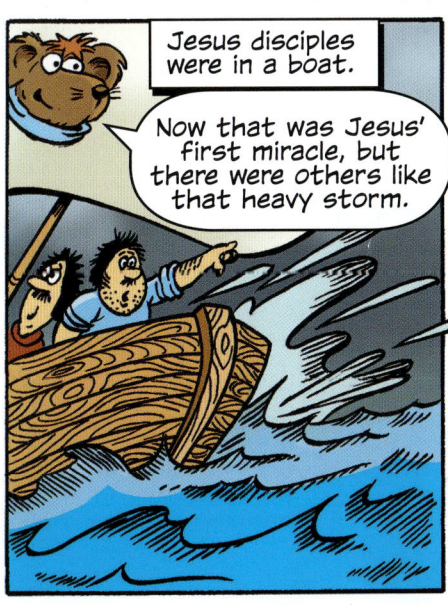

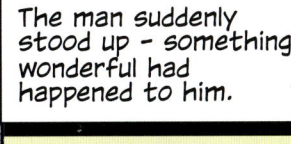